HANUKKAH—THE REAL STORY

THE GUERRILLA WAR FOR NATIONAL LIBERATION AND RELIGIOUS FREEDOM

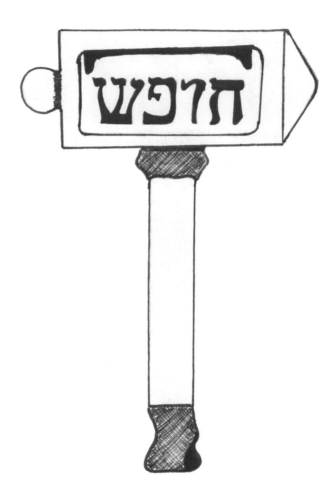

For People of All Races and Religions from 8-98 Years Old

DEDICATION

THIS STORY IS TO HONOR THE JEWISH PEOPLE'S STRUGGLE FOR FREEDOM IN THE PAST, AND TO INSPIRE JEWS TO FIGHT FOR THE LIBERATION OF ALL PEOPLE IN THE PRESENT

THE BOOK OF HANUKKAH - THE REAL STORY
The guerrilla war for national liberation and religious freedom

Storyteller: Paul Harris, co-founder of the San Francisco Community Law Collective, law professor teaching "Guerrilla Lawyering" and author of the critically acclaimed non-fiction book *Black Rage Confronts the Law*

Artist: Vashaun Harris, 19 year old graduate of Oakland School of the Arts

Creative Advisor: Corey Harris, author of *The Tomb of Tupac*
Design and Typography: Josh Harris

Copyright 2020
Center for Guerrilla Law
20 Quickstep Lane, #1,
San Francisco, CA 94115

Contact email: Guerrillalaw@earthlink.net
Copies: Mail check to
Paul Harris at 20 Quickstep Lane, #1,
San Francisco, CA 94115
$16.00 includes book mailing rate or
$20 includes first class mailing

PROLOGUE

How do I know that Hanukkah was the first successful guerrilla war for national liberation and religious freedom in recorded history? It all started with an ancient Book of 8 drawings made by an artist who was actually there in 167 BCE (Before the Christian Empire). This Book's drawings corroborate the story of Hanukkah as it was passed down to me through generations of the Faybusovich and Harris families.

Dear reader please bear with me as I present my family story and then I will retell the story of Hanukkah and produce eight modern copies of the ancient drawings.

Let me take you back to Staradub, a village in Russia near the Ukrainian border. The year is 1905 when Jews suffered terrible pogroms as the Black Hundreds and Cossacks rode through the country killing Jews, burning their homes, destroying and confiscating their property. My grandmother Lena Faybusovich was 15 years old and worked for a nice Gentile couple. When the Cossacks rode through Staradub, this couple hid her in their basement. That night they told her it was safe to flee back home. As she ran through the dark night she tripped over a dead body. Forty years later recounting what happened she trembled as she said, "It was a Jewish man. I can never forget it, all my life." Lena ran on and she found her family in their little home near the outskirts of the village. Their meager possessions had been destroyed. But her father, the wise man of this community, had hid the special book. He called it the "real story of Hanukkah" and each Hanukkah when the family lit the eight candles he carefully took it out and showed the eight drawings of the Maccabean rebellion, preserved for history on the ancient parchment.

In 1910 Lena got ready to leave Russia to join her cousin and fiancé Julius Fine in Chicago. Her father, gravely ill from tuberculosis, gave her the special Book and told her to pass on the real story of Hanukkah to her children and grandchildren. He began to tell her how the family had come into possession of the Book but a violent coughing fit forced him to go to bed. That night the old man passed away.

Lena arrived at Ellis Island and took a train to Chicago where she and Julius were married. They both worked in the garment industry sweatshops of Hart, Shaffner and Marx. In the famous successful strike of 1913 Julius was the spokesperson for the rank-and-file. Lena was arrested with other women picketing for "bread and roses." Their son Moishe (Fred) was on the picket line, arrested and then slapped around by an angry anti-union cop. Julius and Lena were blacklisted from the garment industry.

Years later, Lena gave the Hanukkah Book to her son-in-law Sydney Harris for safe-keeping. Sydney had fought with the Abraham Lincoln Brigade against the fascists in Spain's Civil War in 1938. He had been wounded and spent a year in a prison camp. Upon returning to the United States he became the bodyguard in Chicago for internationally famous African-American concert singer, actor, and socialist, Paul Robeson. Lena was sure that Sydney had the skills to guard the precious Book.

Sydney, who became an esteemed photographer, was also a magnificent storyteller. Every Hanukkah the Harris and Fine/Faybusovich families would light the candles. Sydney would tell the real story of Hanukkah and Lena would show us the ancient eight drawings. On Christmas Eve 1974 the boiler in the Harris house blew up while the family was out celebrating and their home at 1653 N. Sedgwick St. in Chicago burnt down. Thousands of Syd's photos and negatives documenting the social justice history of America were destroyed.

Despondent and overwhelmed Syd did not hunt for the Book. A few weeks later his sons Jerry, Marc, Adam, David, and his daughter Suzanne searched the basement. They found, in a fireproof locker, buried under piles of ashes, hundreds of their father's most valued negatives. And at the bottom of the fireproof locker, wrapped in the original cloth Lena had brought from Russia, was the Book: the real story of Hanukkah.

Sydney was growing old and I was the eldest child. Also, by that time I was a lawyer in San Francisco and a storyteller. The family met and agreed that since I had the experience of defending members of the Black Panthers and anti-war resisters who had come up from the Underground that I had the necessary skills to take possession of the Book; to guard it, and to pass on the story of Hanukkah.

In 1974, Danny and Hillary Goldstine had a tradition of Hanukkah celebrations at their beautiful, large home in Berkeley inviting up to 30 families and providing gifts for children. Danny's mother would tell the traditional story of Hanukkah and I would tell our family version, with the addition of some *magical-political realism*. When my three children reached school age, I would tell our story at their public schools and then every year at Hanukkah gatherings with family and friends. But I was never able to show the ancient drawings in the Book because the parchment was deteriorating from age and I feared they would fall apart. Many years later one of my grandsons, Vashaun Harris, was developing his talents at the Oakland School for the Arts. As he turned 18, I gave him the task of duplicating the eight original ancient drawings. With the artistic assistance of his father Corey and younger sister Kaneasha the drawings were finished in 2020. I committed to writing our story and publishing this book with the new drawings so that all could experience the real story of Hanukkah.

So dear reader, thank you for your patience, and here is
THE BOOK OF HANUKKAH — THE REAL STORY

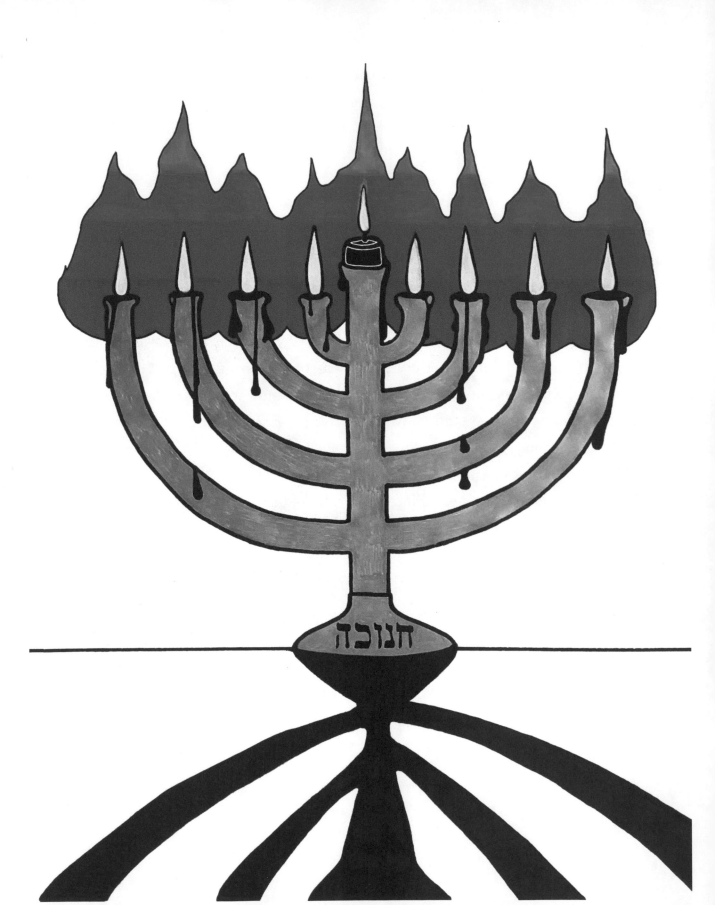

THE BEGINNING

About a hundred and eighty years before baby Jesus was born the Jews lived in a country called Judea (now called Israel). On one of their borders was Syria which was ruled by an evil king named Antiochus Epiphanes, who called himself "God manifest." Syria was considered part of the Seleucid (Greek) Empire and had adopted the Hellenic culture and religion.

One day Antiochus, sitting on his throne, spoke to the famous Greek General Apollonius. "General, these Jews are peaceful people. They are just doctors, lawyers, social workers, and farmers."

Yes, they were farmers; two thousand years later they would write a song praising themselves for this called "Zhankoye."

Now if you look for Paradise
you'll see it there before your eyes
stop your search and go no further on
There we had a collective farm
all run by husky Jewish arms
in Zhankoye, Dzhan, Dzhan, Dzhan

Aunt Natasha drives the tractor
grandma runs the cream extractor
while we work we all can sing our songs
Who says Jews cannot be farmers?
Spit in their eyes! Who would so harm us
Tell them of Zhankoye, Dzhan, Dzhan

Antiochus continued, "They have no Army. You could lead our troops, invade and easily conquer them."

The general responded, "I will prepare our men. We will be in the capital of Jerusalem in a month and occupy their country for the Empire."

Meanwhile in Judea the family of the Maccabees went about their daily life. Their father Mattathias was an old man, but he was still the leader of the Village of Modi'in. His wife had passed and he had five sons. Simon the eldest was a lawyer. Eleazar was a blacksmith and was famous for his huge muscles and a gigantic spear he carried in emergencies. John was a doctor of general medicine with a specialty in emergency surgery. Judah was smart, handsome and a star soccer player. Jonathan, the youngest, was 16 and something of a *rebel without a cause.*

The brothers did not know that over 2000 years later they would still be remembered as Heroes of liberation. *And America's famous novelist of historical-fiction, Howard Fast, would write a best-seller entitled My Glorious Brothers, recreating their liberation struggle.*

DESECRATION OF THE TEMPLE

One Sunday morning Jonathan rode his black stallion named Gesundheit over to his cousin Rose's house. Rose took her horse, Flame, named for his golden mane, and they trotted off for a day in Jerusalem, unaware that within hours their lives and the fate of the Jewish people would change forever.

Entering the city they saw Syrian soldiers on each street corner. Hiding their horses in the woods on the outskirts they crept through the alleyways until they reached the Temple. Daredevils that they were, they climbed almost to the top of the Temple and watched with horror the scene below. The Temple was filled with soldiers who were desecrating it. The Torah had been ripped to pieces. The Menorah had been thrown to the ground and the olive oil which provided the constant and eternal light had been spilled out of it.

The Jews had been lined up against the wall. The Greek Commander called the rabbi forward. "Go forth to your fellow rabbis and to your people and tell them from now on we are confiscating your lands. Your schools will be closed; anyone teaching from the Torah will be executed. You must renounce your foolish belief in one God and pray to our many Gods. You will pay our administrator taxes and live under our rules."

The rabbi fled, going directly to the city's formal leadership. These religious leaders and wealthy men agreed that resistance was futile and their only path was one of acceptance and hopefully of compromise with the occupiers.

THE BEGINNING

About a hundred and eighty years before baby Jesus was born the Jews lived in a country called Judea (now called Israel). On one of their borders was Syria which was ruled by an evil king named Antiochus Epiphanes, who called himself "God manifest." Syria was considered part of the Seleucid (Greek) Empire and had adopted the Hellenic culture and religion.

One day Antiochus, sitting on his throne, spoke to the famous Greek General Apollonius. "General, these Jews are peaceful people. They are just doctors, lawyers, social workers, and farmers."

Yes, they were farmers; two thousand years later they would write a song praising themselves for this called "Zhankoye."

Now if you look for Paradise
you'll see it there before your eyes
stop your search and go no further on
There we had a collective farm
all run by husky Jewish arms
in Zhankoye, Dzhan, Dzhan, Dzhan

Aunt Natasha drives the tractor
grandma runs the cream extractor
while we work we all can sing our songs
Who says Jews cannot be farmers?
Spit in their eyes! Who would so harm us
Tell them of Zhankoye, Dzhan, Dzhan

Antiochus continued, "They have no Army. You could lead our troops, invade and easily conquer them."

The general responded, "I will prepare our men. We will be in the capital of Jerusalem in a month and occupy their country for the Empire."

Meanwhile in Judea the family of the Maccabees went about their daily life. Their father Mattathias was an old man, but he was still the leader of the Village of Modi'in. His wife had passed and he had five sons. Simon the eldest was a lawyer. Eleazar was a blacksmith and was famous for his huge muscles and a gigantic spear he carried in emergencies. John was a doctor of general medicine with a specialty in emergency surgery. Judah was smart, handsome and a star soccer player. Jonathan, the youngest, was 16 and something of a *rebel without a cause.*

The brothers did not know that over 2000 years later they would still be remembered as Heroes of liberation. *And America's famous novelist of historical-fiction, Howard Fast, would write a best-seller entitled My Glorious Brothers, recreating their liberation struggle.*

Back at the Temple the soldiers had put up a huge statue of the Greek God Zeus. The Lieutenant brought out a dead boar. Placing it on a pedestal he said sarcastically, "This is one of our Gods. You must bow down to it." No one moved. The soldier grabbed a young man and forced him to his knees, commanding him to bow down to the bleeding boar. The young man refused. He then looked to his mother Hannah who gestured for him to remain strong and stay silent. One by one, Hannah's other five sons refused to pray to the dead pig, and were put in handcuffs. Hannah's last son, only 8 years old, was called forward.

"Bow to your new God!"

The boy replied, "That's not a God, it's a pig…Pig!"

The soldier slapped the little boy and ordered that he and his five brothers were to be separated from their mother and taken to the juvenile detention center set up by the Greek Security Forces.

Rose and Jonathan could not stand watching anymore. They rapelled down the Temple's wall, ran through the back alleys of Jerusalem to their horses and rode back to Modi'in to tell Mattathias what was happening. As they galloped through their land, they shouted at the people in every hamlet and village, "The Syrians are coming, the soldiers are coming!"

THE NEXT DAY IN MODI'IN

After securing Jerusalem, General Apollonius, expecting no resistance, sent out small bands of soldiers to post the new rules of occupation in every village. Into Modi'in rode nine soldiers with a wagon. Their swords were drawn, they were laughing and swearing and acting as all bullies act, even in our modern times. They had the Mayor gather all the Jews into the large Town Square. They nailed the Rules of Occupation to the wooden walls of the village Temple. The rules were clear.

1. No teaching from the Torah.
2. No praying to the Hebrew false god.
3. Compulsory attendance at the Greek schools.
4. All temples shut down.
5. Curfew one hour after sundown.
6. Groups of three or more Jews will be prosecuted for the *crime of Conspiracy to Commit Criminal Anarchy.*
7. 60% of your farm produce to be paid to the tax collector.
8. 60% of all business receipts will be paid to the tax collector.

The Captain had two of his soldiers unload the statue in their wagon. It was a 10 foot statue of the Greek God of War, Ares. He called the Mayor forward. "Kneel and pray to your new God." The Mayor began to shake with fright; in the crowd people yelled "No, don't do it!" The Captain raised his voice, "On your knees, bow your head and pray!" Mattathias and his sons had moved to the front of the crowd. "Mattathias, please stop the sacrilege," pleaded the Elders of Modi'in. The Captain shouted, "Renounce your God! Renounce your false, foolish and blasphemous religion! Bow and pray!"

As the Mayor fell to his knees, Mattathias moved forward, "*If there is one thing I cannot abide it is an Uncle Tom, a Tio Taco, or an Uncle Schwartz.*" With one powerful stroke of his ancient, blessed sword he cut off the Mayor's head. The crowd rushed forward, knocking down the statue. The outnumbered and frightened soldiers, no longer supported by their false bravado, ran to their horses and fled.

THE NIGHT OF THE HAMMER

That night Mattathias called his sons and their cousin Rose together. His already weakened heart was skipping abnormally causing him to speak softly. *Two thousand years from now an American folk singer, Pete Seeger, will put these same words from the Bible to a song.* "I want you to listen to these words now."

> To everything, turn turn turn, there is a season, turn turn turn,
> And a time to every purpose under heaven.
> A time to be born, a time to die. A time to plant, a time to reap.
> A time to kill, a time to heal. A time to laugh, a time to weep.
> A time for every purpose under heaven.
> A time of love, a time of hate. A time of war, a time of peace...

"My family, this is now a time of war. We must prepare a guerrilla war."

"But there are no gorillas in Judea," said Jonathan.

Judah laughed, "A guerrilla war is when the few, with the support of the many, organize against the mighty and privileged. *Like Frodo and Sam in The Fellowship of the Ring; like Tom Paine in the American Revolution; like Che Guevara and Fidel in Cuba; like Ho Chi Minh in Vietnam; like Nelson Mandela and the African National Congress in South Africa; like Robin Hood in Sherwood Forest.*"

Mattathias asked Eleazar to bring a huge chest from the storeroom. *Opening it he took out two books: "Revolution in the Revolution" by the 20th century Frenchman Regis Debray and "Book of Five Rings" by Japan's greatest Samurai, Miyamoto Musashi.* "Study these books of guerrilla warfare."

Then he took out five war hammers and a shining sword. He handed each of his sons a hammer.

"We are the Maccabee, which means 'the hammer.' Each one is inscribed with the Yiddish word Freiheit (freedom)." He then gave the sword to Rose.

"Tomorrow you will organize a guerrilla force
and move into the forest and hills between
Modi'in and Jerusalem.
You will take back our country and protect
our religion and culture.
I am weary now and must go to sleep.
I love you all."
Later that night the old wise man's
heart gave out, and he passed from
the suffering and beauty of their
world.

The next day Rose and the brothers
began to recruit. They went door-to-
door trying to persuade their neighbors
to join with them, but had little success.
The day after that, Simon called the
villagers to the Town Square.
Judah picked a 13 year old boy
out of the crowd. "Close your
thumb and don't let me
pull it open."

The boy, proud that Judah had chosen him, closed his thumb tightly. Judah easily pried it open. "The thumb was all alone; this time close your thumb and the index finger." But again he pulled them open easily. Judah told the boy to close all of his fingers into a fist. The boy made a tight fist with all his might and Judah could not pull them open. Judah held up his own fist and shouted, "You see what happens when we are no longer alone; when we join together we are strong, we are invincible!" A teacher in the crowd named Esther sang out "*El Pueblo Unido, Jamas Sera Vencido.* The People United Will Never Be Defeated." The people of the village joined Esther; young and old men, women and children singing together. The Guerrilla War had taken its first step.

INTO THE HILLS

Over the next three months the Maccabees recruited hundreds of their people and a few Arabs who lived in Judea and resented the occupation of the Seleucid Empire. The guerrilla camps were organized with each unit led by a Maccabee brother.

John the doctor opened four small field hospitals which were the People's Free Clinics.

Eleazar the blacksmith rounded up his fellow artisans and began producing spears, bows, arrows, long and short swords, shields and light armor.

Simon the lawyer was elected Chief Judge and he created the People's Courts. Each tribunal had one person over 55 years old for their experience, one person under 25 for the perspective of youth, and one lawyer or trained arbitrator. Their purpose was to solve the conflicts and disagreements inside the guerrilla camps. *They studied two books: one by internationally respected Arbitrator Ken Cloke, titled "Conflict Resolution" and the other by Mao Zedong, "On the Correct Handling of the Contradictions Among the People."* In addition, Simon instituted a gentler form of criticism, self-criticism sessions which proved valuable in building honesty, self-reflection and unity among the guerrillas.

Jonathan opened a Recreation Center where the many young adults and teenagers would play soccer, skateboard and practice the self defense art of krav maga.

Rose set up Freedom Schools where the Torah and books of neighboring peoples were read and discussed. Esther organized cultural nights where each camp would gather in the evening, singing, dancing the Hora, performing spoken word stories and stand up comedy which was so ingrained in Jewish culture.

Judah trained those who volunteered for the fighting and developed tactics and strategy with the guerrilla leadership.

ATTACK

For two years, small courageous bands of Jews attacked the Syrian military outposts and police stations. Each target was chosen carefully and with each success they were able to confiscate the weapons and often the plans of the Empire's puppets. Their confidence grew; their numbers grew. Their enemies became scared and desertions among the occupiers became a serious problem. This was especially true after the Maccabees defeated General Apollonias and Judah took his sword, which he then used throughout the battles. The next year they gained a major victory when they defeated the Syrian Governor Seron who used the traditional formation of the Phalanx which proved unwieldy and ineffective against the hit-and-run Guerrilla tactics.

In 165 BCE Antiochus called General Lysias to his Palace. "This revolt must be destroyed now. Don't talk. No excuses. Listen. *I have been reading the Handbook for United States Forces in Vietnam and now I understand why you have been losing. General W.C. Westmoreland writes-- 'The guerrilla forces are challenging us with new fighting techniques.' The Handbook warns in Section III to 'be cautious of all civilians.'* Your problem Lysias is that the Maccabees are supported by the people of Judea. They are like the fish; the people are like the ocean."

"General, we don't have 'anti-personnel weapons such as napalm and fragmentation bombs' listed in the Handbook. But the good news is that the Greek Empire is sending us five Monsters. You will use these Demons of Death and you will subdue the civilian population which is supporting the Maccabees and then obliterate these terrorists."

THE NIGHT OF FEAR

Judah's Arab allies in Syria had warned him about the approaching invasion. He gave his two best scouts, Jonathan and Rose, the responsibility to ride out and see where Lysias had positioned his army and what was the basis of the rumors about the "monsters." Riding through the forest Jonathan and Rose saw the army near the mouth of the canyon. Tying their horses near the river they crept close enough to see clearly. "Oh, no! They do have five monsters," whispered Jonathan. Just then, two sentries spotted them. Jonathan and Rose ran to their horses. "Johnny, no horse is as fast as Flame. So I'll draw their attention and they'll follow me. You go back through the forest and warn Judah."

Flame galloped along the riverbank as the two sentries rode after Rose, hurling threats of death. Flame, who came from a long line of Arabians (the finest race horses) was not only fast but also was a great jumper. Into the water Rose guided Flame and urged him to jump the large fallen log blocking the outer bank. Successfully making the jump that the Syrian war horses were unable to do, Rose was able to lose the soldiers and make it back to the Maccabee Encampment.

Meanwhile, Jonathan had ridden into camp, dismounted and burst into the command center where Judah was planning their dawn attack. His body shaking, Jonathan reported, "They have about 1,000 troops at the edge of the canyon and five monsters. We are doomed."

"Calm down Johnny," said Simon, putting his hands on his youngest brother's shoulders. "Describe these monsters."

"They are about 10 ft tall, dark gray color, giant floppy ears, a nose five feet long, huge legs and feet like tree trunks and white spears growing out of their mouths."

Simon and the others laughed. "Johnny, you should have spent more time in zoology class. Those are not demons or monsters, they are just normal large mammals. They're elephants."

Simon continued, " The four of them will be led by a bull elephant. Lysias will probably ride on top of it. Elephants can be trained to go into war, but it's not natural to them. If the bull falls from our arrows and spears the other elephants will run away."

Judah was emboldened by Jonathan's report. He called together his people. "At dawn we will attack. Rachel and Eli will take our first brigade and start to harass the Syrians as the sun begins to rise. This will draw them closer to the mouth of the canyon. They know they outnumber us and with the elephants they will be overconfident. I will let them see me. They will try to capture me and make the mistake of entering the canyon. Moishe and Esther and our archery brigade will be on both sides of the cliffs raining hundreds of arrows down upon them. David and Malka will leave early in the night and with their brigade creep through our tunnels in the valley until they are located behind the troops. Once their troops are trapped in the canyon Eleazar and Shoshanna's brigade will attack from the front."

As the men, women and teenagers gathered closer together Judah gave his final speech. "My brothers and sisters, we have been together many years now. If any of you want to return home to your families tonight do so without shame or regret. Those of you who are conscientious objectors get the field hospitals ready for the wounded. The rest of you try to sleep, for tomorrow we will win back Judea and ride into Jerusalem a free people."

THE BATTLE

At first the strategy was successful. But as boxing champ *Mike Tyson has said, "Everyone has a good plan until they get smashed in the mouth."* The elephants frightened the Jews and some of them began to retreat in panic. Eleazar knew a dramatic action had to be taken. Lifting his 10 foot spear he rushed to meet the bull elephant upon which General Lysias sat leading the enemy troops. He stood under its huge body stabbing the spear deep into its heart. The elephant fell onto his front knees and Lysias was thrown to the ground. But the elephant's mighty trunk knocked Eleazar down and as the elephant fell forward its body crushed the courageous Maccabee.

Three things happened, one right after another. First, the other four elephants threw their riders off, turned and ran out of the canyon to the plains where they felt safe. Second, the Jews, encouraged by the flight of the elephants, enraged by Eleazar's death, and fortified by their comrade's sacrifice, renewed their attacks from front and back. Third, Lysias was captured. This, along with the elephants leaving and the dynamic attack of the Jews spread despair among the Syrian troops and what was left of their Greek commanders. Within an hour they had fled or surrendered. Judah sent General Lysias back to Antiochus with a message tied around his neck: NEVER AGAIN.

CLEANING THE TEMPLE

Among cries of *"Hasta la Victoria Siempre" (Until the final Victory)* the Guerrilla Army marched towards Jerusalem. People from the villages and towns joined the parade and celebration. But when they entered the Temple they were shocked by the sight of their precious religious symbols and relics broken on the ground, overshadowed by a gigantic statue of the Greek God Zeus. Judah walked to the center of this abominable mess and commanded the people, "Go to the River Jordan: fill pails with sand and freshwater. Come back to the Temple and cleanse it three times."

Rabbi Adler, who had taught at the Freedom School motioned to Judah, "Look, there is only a small bit of oil left in the menorah. The light is supposed to shine always but this will last only one or two days. Where can we obtain fresh oil? The Greeks confiscated all our menorahs and oil."

Jamal, Eleazar's lieutenant, said there was a Bedouin camp where he had relatives. It was a hundred miles from Jerusalem; they hated the occupation and had barrels of olive oil they would trade.

Johnathan came forward and said, "At our encampments Jamal and I were in charge of training for long distance running. We can run to the Bedouin camp and return in eight days."

In America in the 1860's a Native American leader, Geronimo, and his Apache tribe members, men, women, and children trained like marathon runners. He and his band would attack a military outpost which occupied their lands and then they would run 25 miles to a hideout.

"Sounds crazy, but since Gesundheit and Flame were wounded and need to recover, it's our only alternative" said Rose.
Jonathan and Jamal went to the peaceful garden behind the Temple and meditated deeply for an hour. Then taking flasks of water, pieces of salt and *chocolate gelt* to exchange for the oil, they jogged out of the city.

In the guerrilla camp, Johnathan and Jamal had listened to the music of folksingers *Jerry Atinsky* and *Jasmin Levy*, as well as *Bobby Zimmerman* and *Carole King*. They especially liked the raps of *San Francisco Street Music*.

A particular lyric the children at the recreation center loved ran through their minds as they trudged over the sands:

I'm Vashaun I'm strong like a tree

We love hip hop and hip hop loves me

I'm Kaneasha I shine like a leaf

We love hip hop and hip hop loves me

I'm Orion I grow like a seed

We love hip hop and hip hop loves me

Three cousins our roots run deep

We love hip hop and hip hop loves me

BROTHER AND SISTERHOOD

Running 25 miles every 24 hours in the heat was too exhausting, so the young men would start to run in the evening and run all night and at dawn find shelter, sleep, wake, repeat. Along the way people gave them fruit, matzoh, and water.

Meanwhile, the first day and night the oil burned brightly and there was a light in the Temple. The second and third days and nights, to everyone's amazement, the oil continued to burn and provide the sacred light.

The last 25 miles through the scorching desert were difficult but the young men ran on, while in Jerusalem on the fourth day the oil was still burning. Reaching the Bedouin camp in the late morning Jamal was greeted as a hero and Jonathan was treated as a friend, for the tribe had heard of the Maccabees' victory. That evening there was a celebration with delicious meals, singing and dancing. For the first time the two boys were able to sleep securely and wake refreshed. In the morning Jamal's father gave him the precious oil. In a solemn ceremony Jamal presented it to Jonathan who felt the presence of his father Mattathias standing behind him. He poured the oil into two flasks and with the flasks tied to their waists the two young men started the four day journey home.

They ran through the desert not knowing that the oil in the Temple was still burning on the fifth day and night. They ran over the hills as the oil burned less brightly on the sixth day yet continued through that night.

Inside the Temple, Rose and Malka sat by the menorah as the flame flickered.

"Do you think it will go out before they return?" asked Rose.

"I am surprised that it has lasted this long. But I have faith it will continue to shine until the boys get back."

"Do you think history will remember us, what we sacrificed and what we achieved?" Rose quietly asked.

"I know that Hanukkah songs will be written, rituals created, and celebrations will take place every year. Rosie, even if no one remembers us, I know it was worth it."

In a loud, clear voice Rose responded, "The last three years have given me purpose, freedom and love. I have no regrets, and I never will."

Rosie the teenager and Malka the young mother hugged each other in camaraderie and the flickering flame seemed to grow and dance inside the Temple walls.

The two 19 year old boys, hardened by three years of revolt, continued on their mission. Their calves tightening, their ankles swelling, their quadriceps throbbing, they pushed themselves beyond exhaustion under the unforgiving heat of Judea's sun as the oil in the Temple burned less and less brightly.

On the eighth morning the boys continued to run, their lips parched, their feet blistered, their lungs crying out for air. They ran and ran as the light in the menorah began to sputter out. At noon on the eighth day our courageous young men stumbled into the Temple. John had them lie down and began to treat them. Simon took the oil to the menorah. Rabbi Adler poured in the oil and the light shined brightly throughout the cleansed and restored temple.

People filled the temple and others massed together outside. Judah spoke to the crowd. "A miracle happened here. Now we will forge a menorah which will hold 9 candles. Each year we will gather with friends and family. We will take the shamash from the middle of the menorah and we'll light one candle each day. And each person who lights a candle will do it in honor of someone or something they love."

The people joined hands in gratitude and joy and sang, *We Shall Overcome*!

THE MIRACLE

Some say the oil burned eight days because it was enchanted. Some say it was because the oil happened to be of extraordinary quality. Some say God kept it burning because Jews are the chosen people. Isn't the true miracle that a people rose up against all odds, liberated their country, reestablished their religion and built a culture of freedom?

EPILOGUE

Every Hanukkah our family gets together: the Faybusoviches from Russia, the Santiagos from Brazil, the Henriquezes from El Salvador, the Newmans from Sweden, the Harrises from Scotland and England. Jamie Carmen says the blessing. Each child lights a candle for someone they love or for a wish they hold dear. The youngest lit a candle on the 4th night in the Hebrew year 5780 (2020). "For whom do you light the candle, child?" The little girl answered, "For peace between the Jewish and Palestinian peoples."